PENGUIN BOOKS

PUNOGRAPHY TOO

Bruce A. McMillan was born in Boston, grew up in Maine, and earned his B.S. degree in biology at the University of Maine in 1969. He has worked as a television producer-director and an island caretaker—spending two years with his wife, Terry, and son, Brett, as the sole year-round residents on a Maine island. He now devotes his time to photography and writing. In addition to *Punography* (also published by Penguin Books) and *Punography Too*, Mr. McMillan is the author of five photographic books for young readers: *Finestkind o' Day: Lobstering in Maine; The Alphabet Symphony; The Remarkable Riderless Runaway Tricycle; Apples, How They Grow;* and *Making Sneakers.* He lives with his family at a secluded spot in Shapleigh, Maine.

The bookplate

PUNOGRAPHY TOO

BRUCE A. McMILLAN

PENGUIN BOOKS

Penguin Books Ltd, Harmondsworth,
Middlesex, England
Penguin Books, 625 Madison Avenue,
New York, New York 10022, U.S.A.
Penguin Books Australia Ltd, Ringwood,
Victoria, Australia
Penguin Books Canada Limited, 2801 John Street,
Markham, Ontario, Canada L3R 1B4
Penguin Books (N.Z.) Ltd, 182–190 Wairau Road,
Auckland 10, New Zealand

First published 1980
Reprinted 1981

LIBRARY OF CONGRESS CATALOGING IN PUBLICATION DATA
McMillan, Bruce A.
Punography too.
1. American wit and humor, Pictorial. I. Title.
NC1429.M265A4 1980 779 80-15116
ISBN 0 14 00.5666 1

Printed in the United States of America by
Capital City Press, Inc., Montpelier, Vermont
Set in Helvetica

For Ed and Eleanor of Rauhamaa Farm

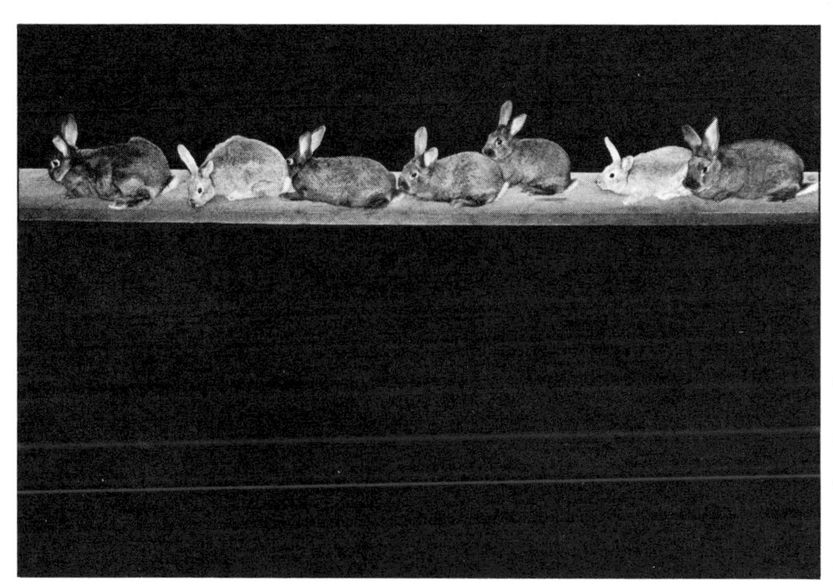

A receding hareline

A light smoker

Reading between the lions

He beets around the bush.

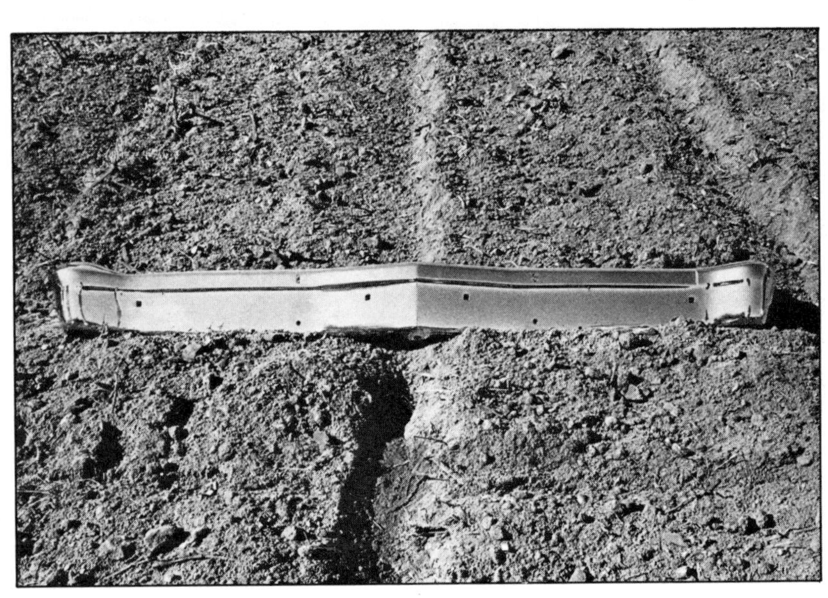

A bumper crop

Outstanding in his field

Laying it on the line

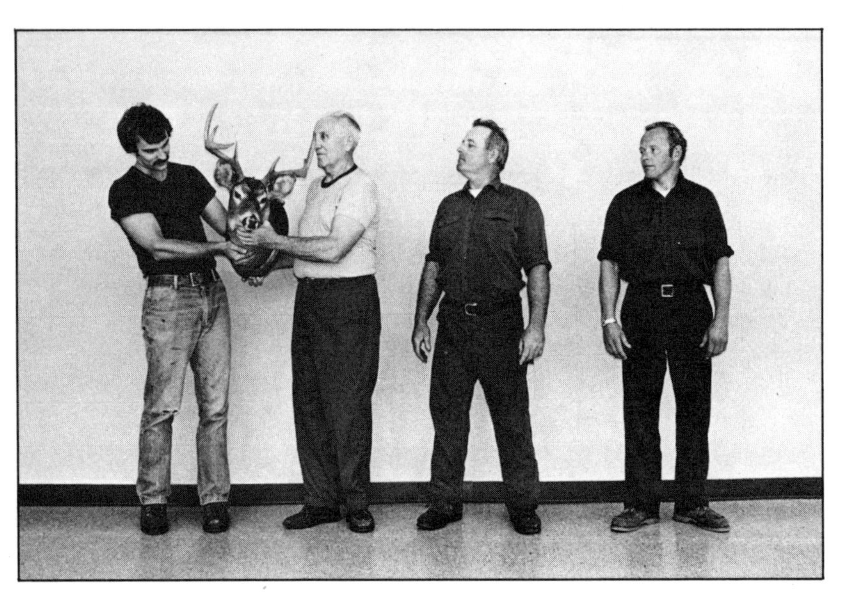

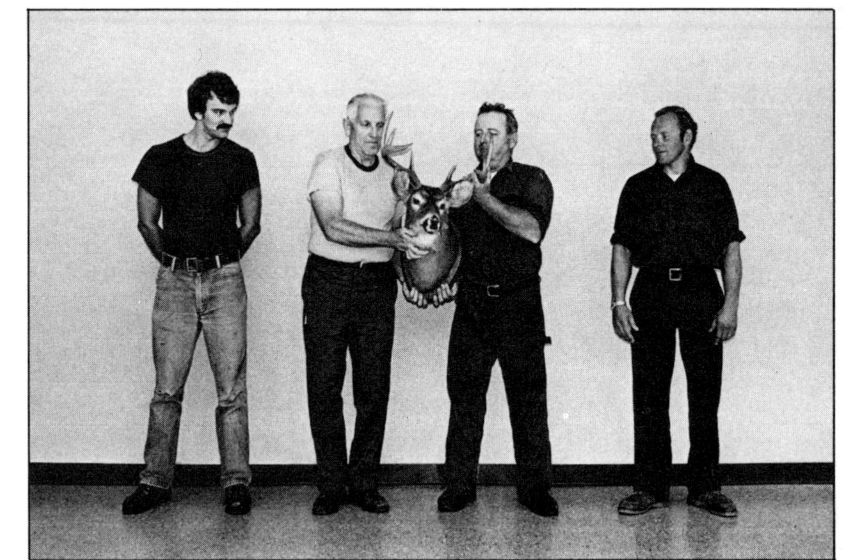

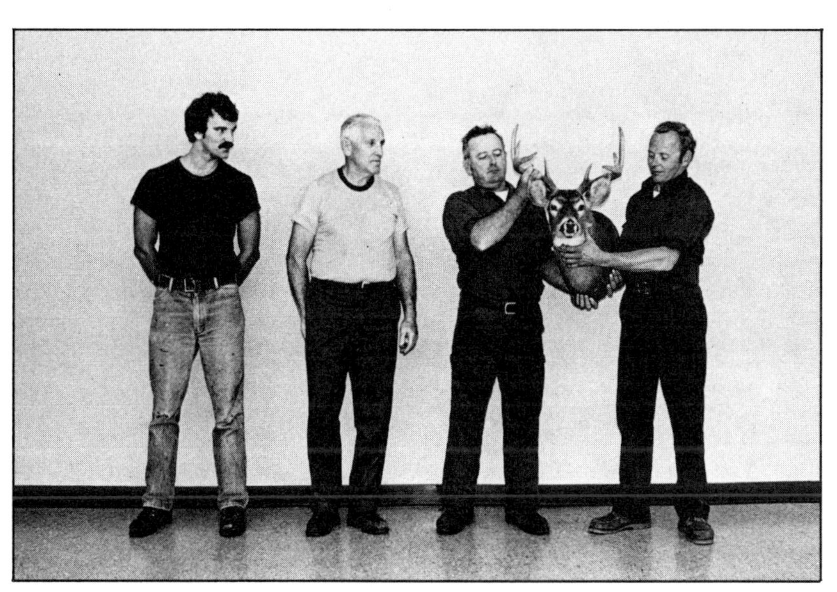

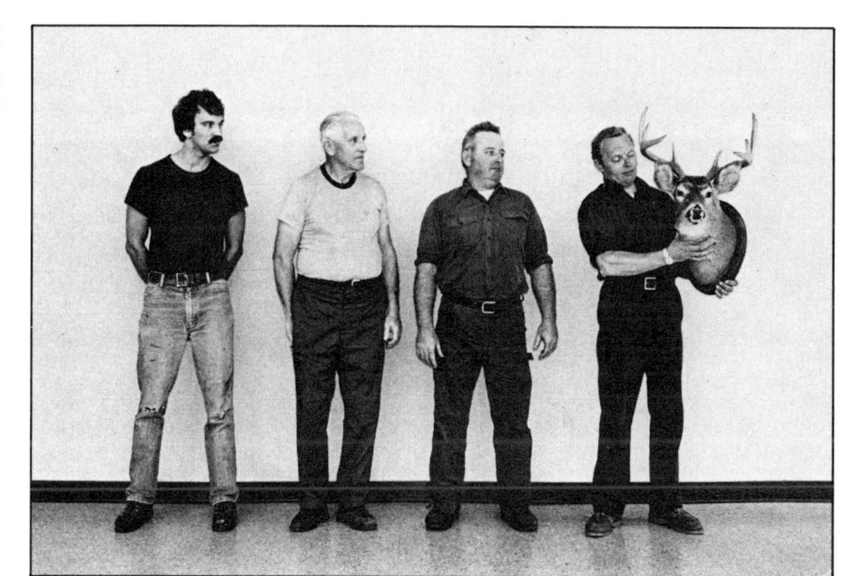

Passing the buck

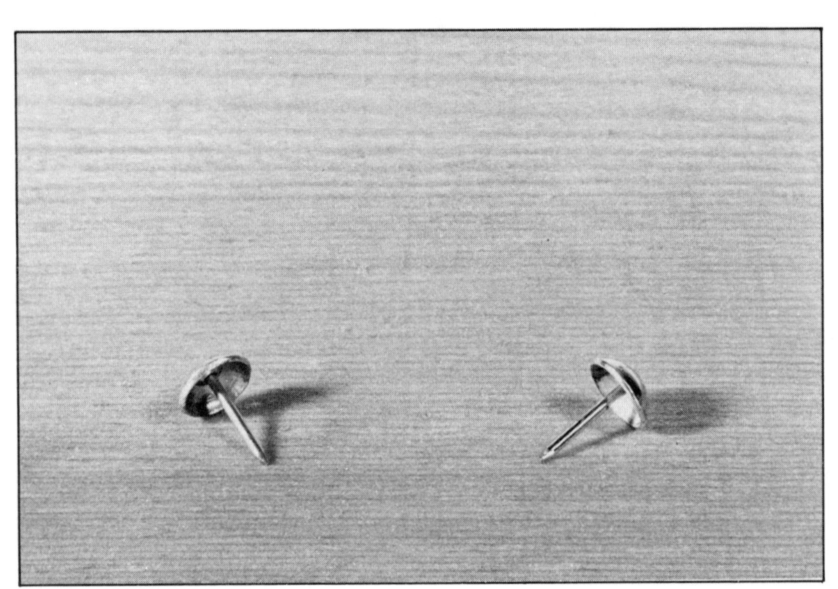

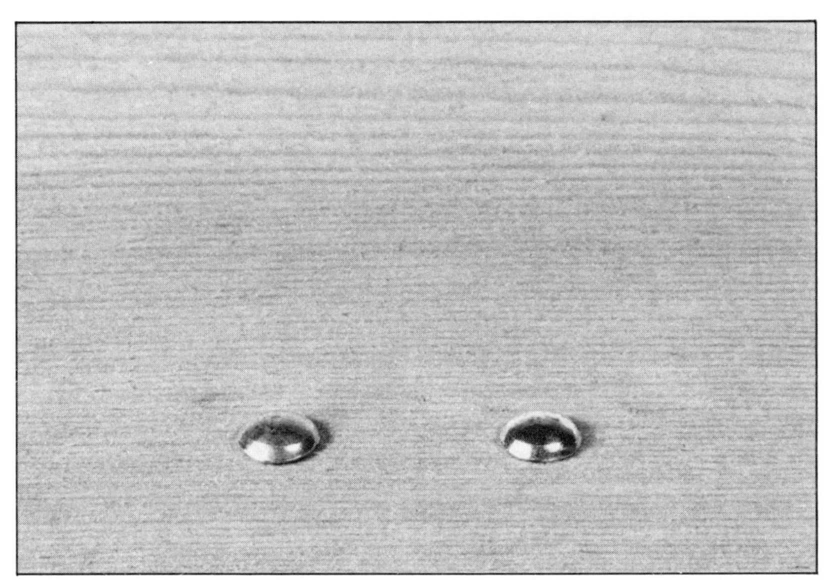

Getting down two brass tacks

Frank 'n' stein

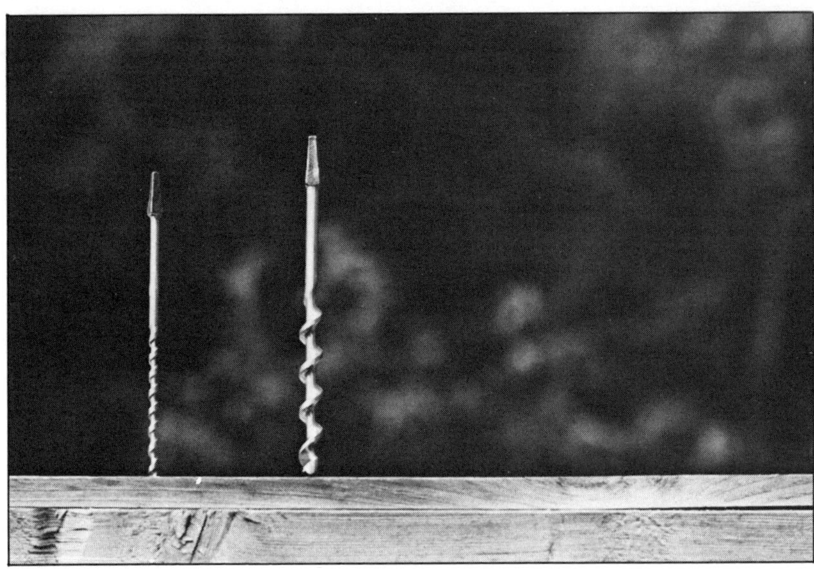

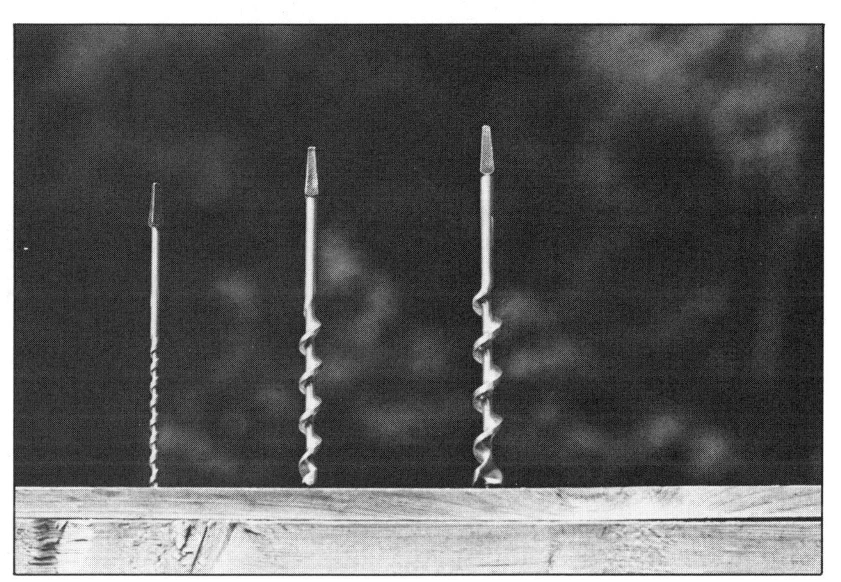

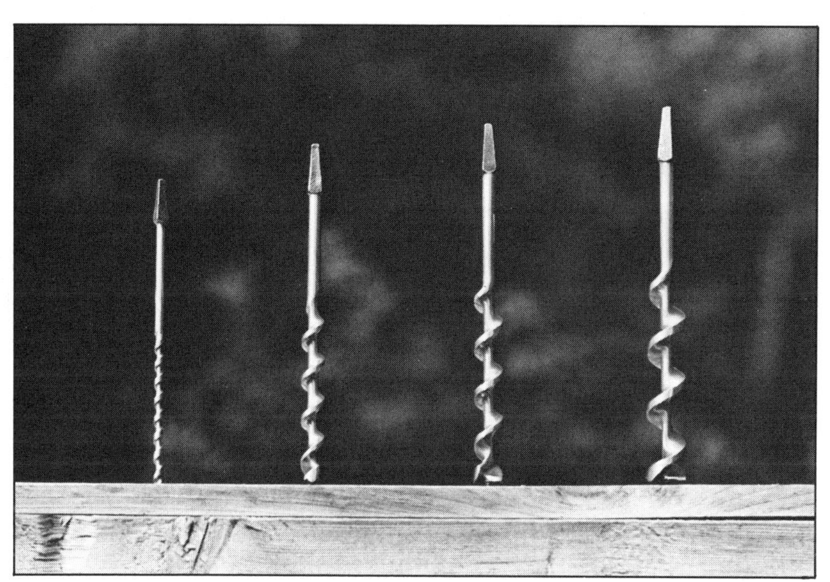

Bit by bit by bit by bit

Two go off on a tan gent.

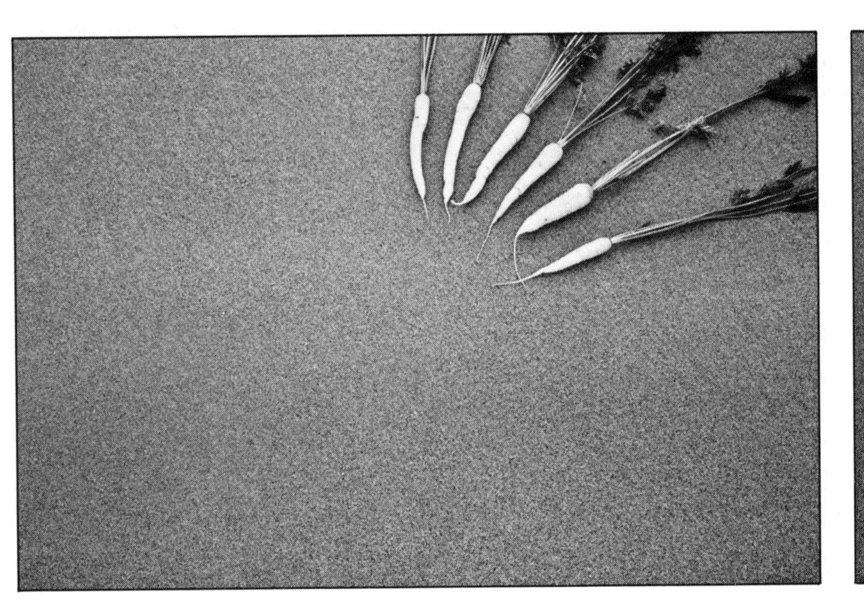

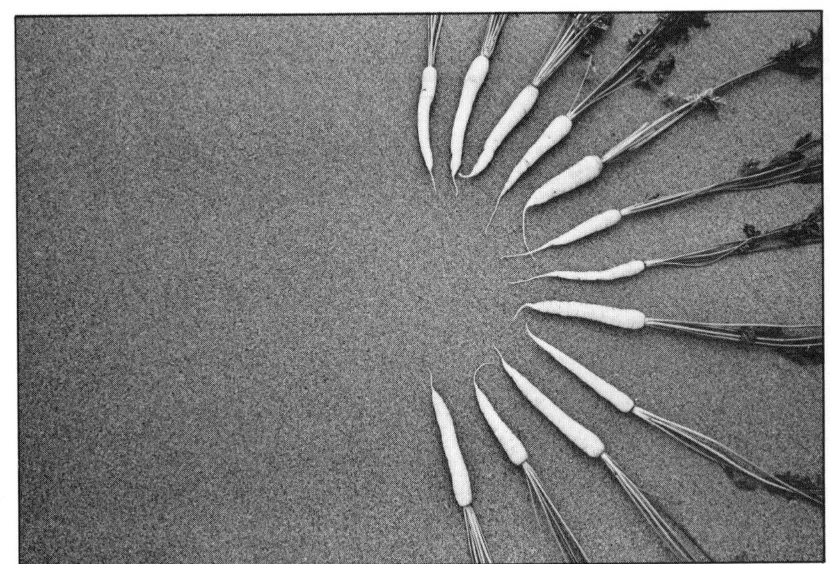

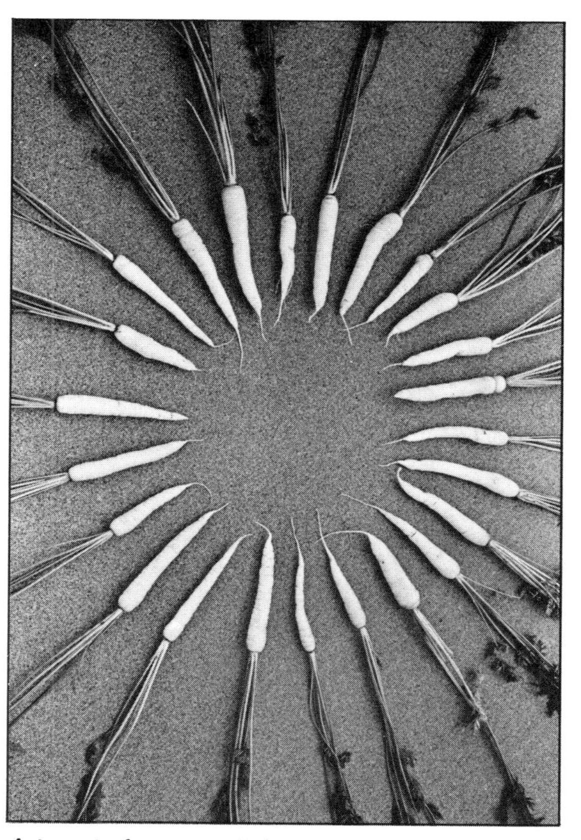

A twenty-four carrot ring

AMERICAN

A real swinging pear

Changing attire

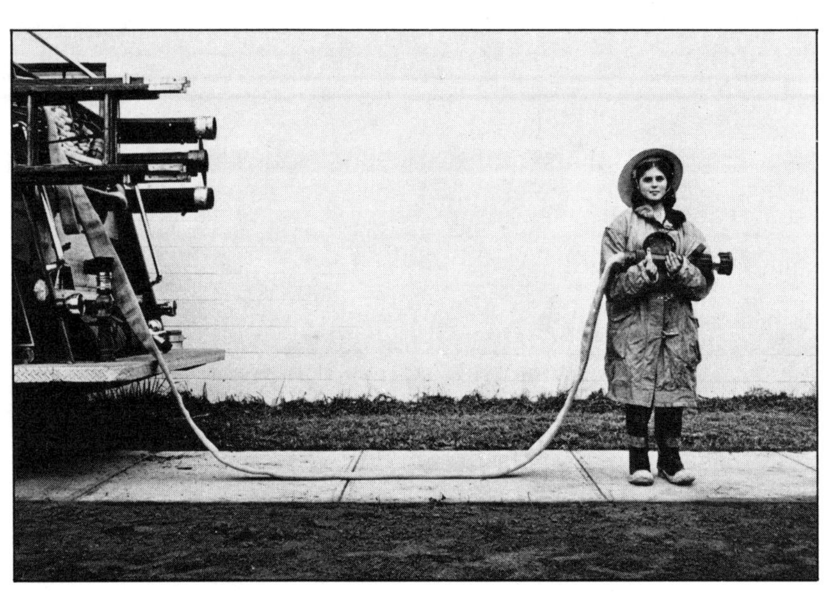

Ladies support hose.

The belle of the ball

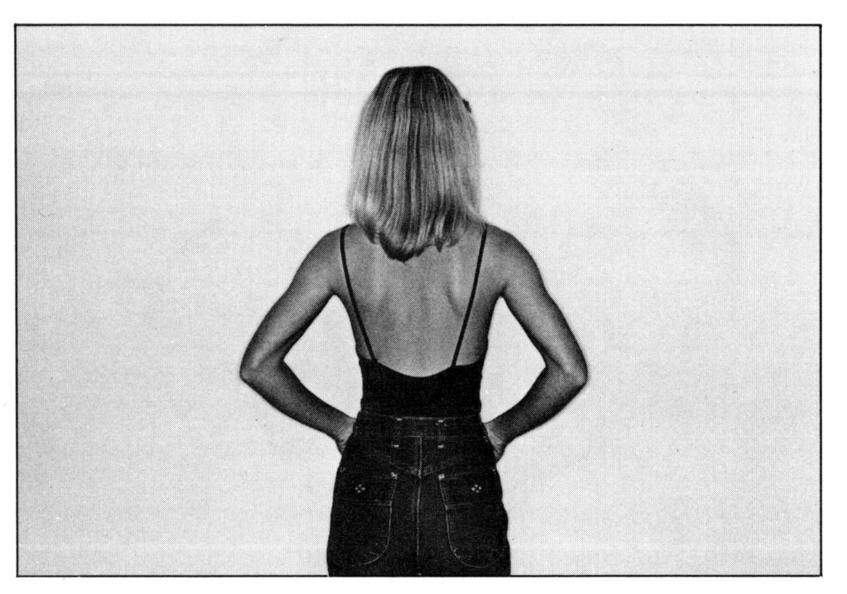

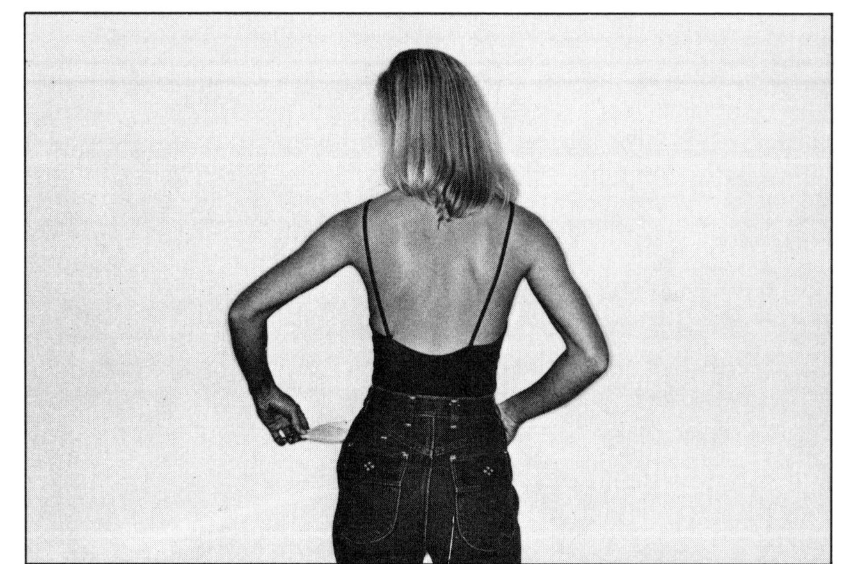

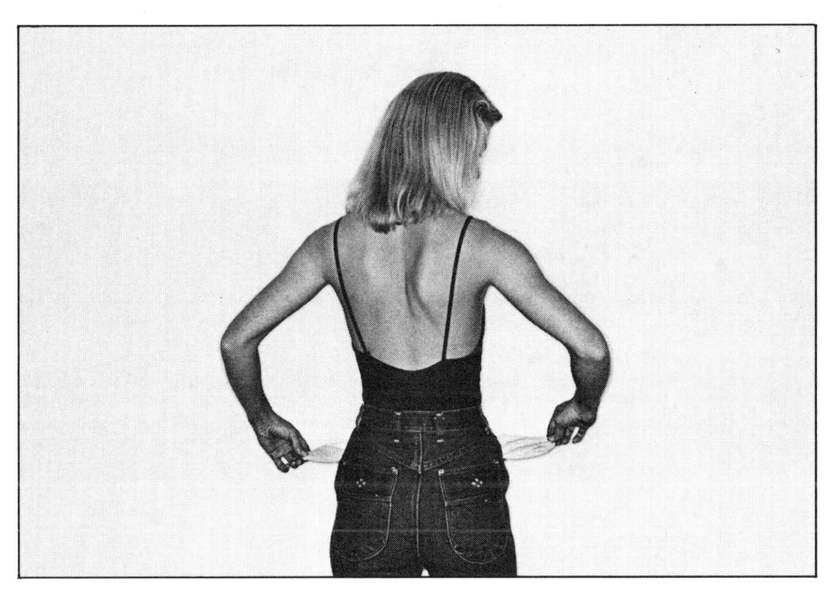

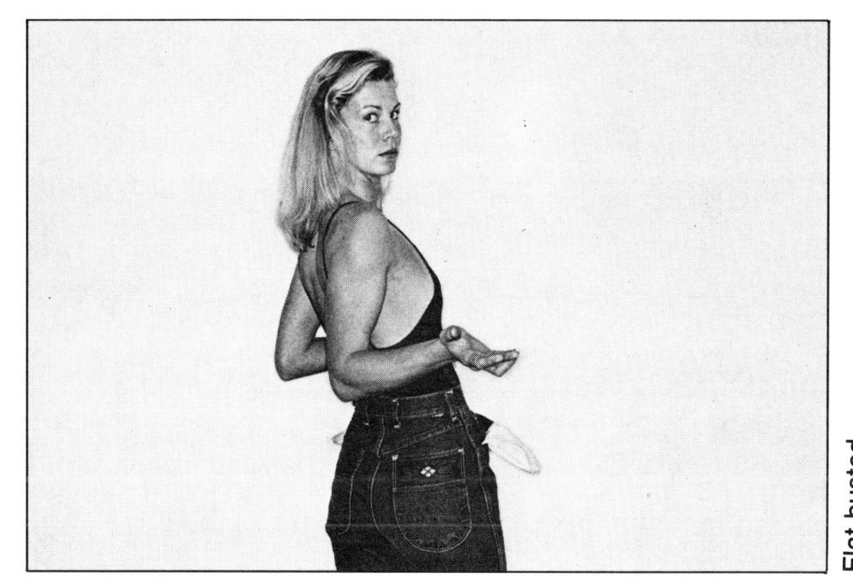

Flat busted

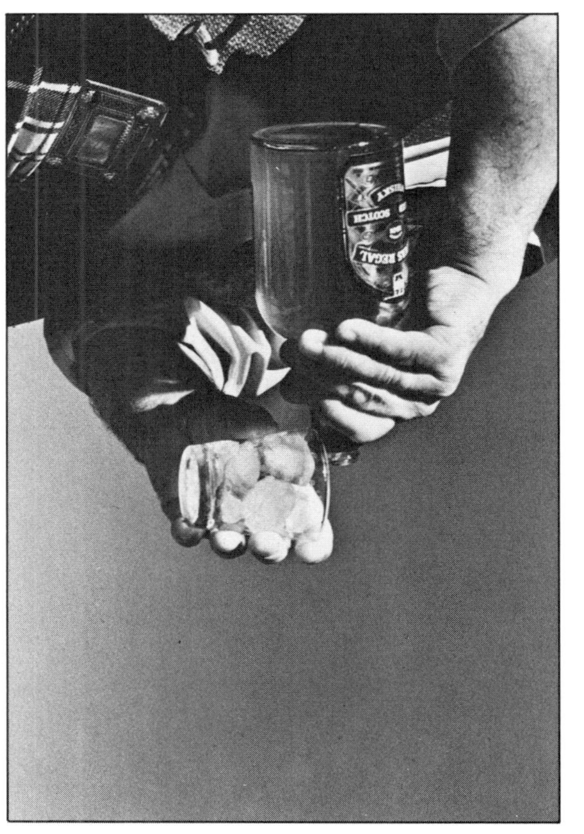

Scotch on the rocks

Rock and roll

B
cresc.
C
D
E
cresc.

B
cresc.
C
D
E
cresc.

A string quartet

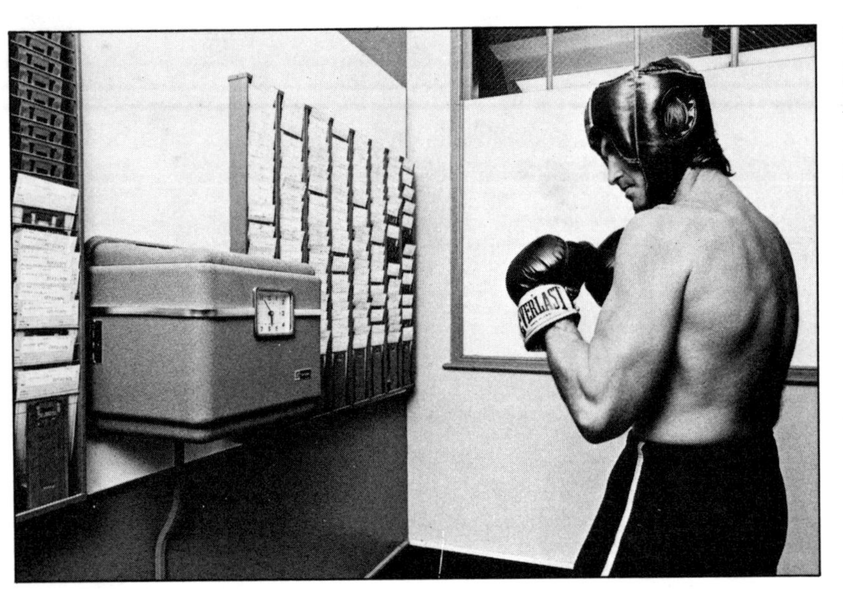
EVERLAST

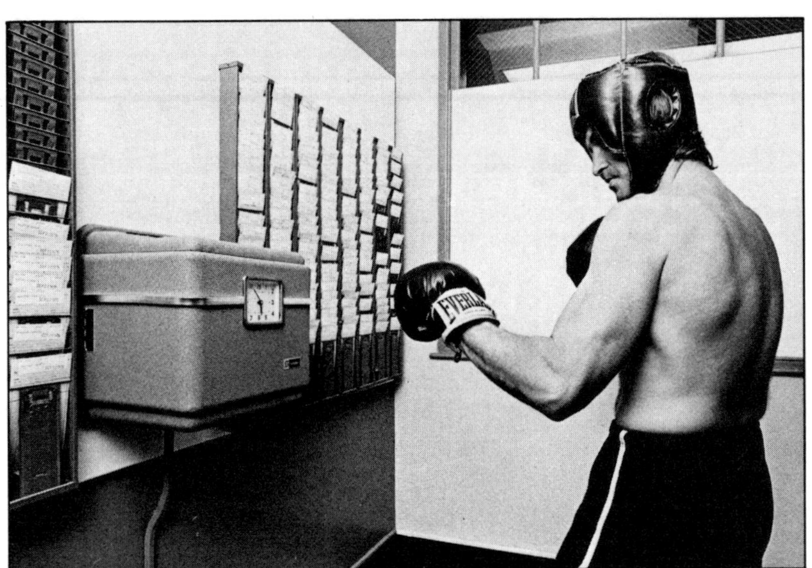

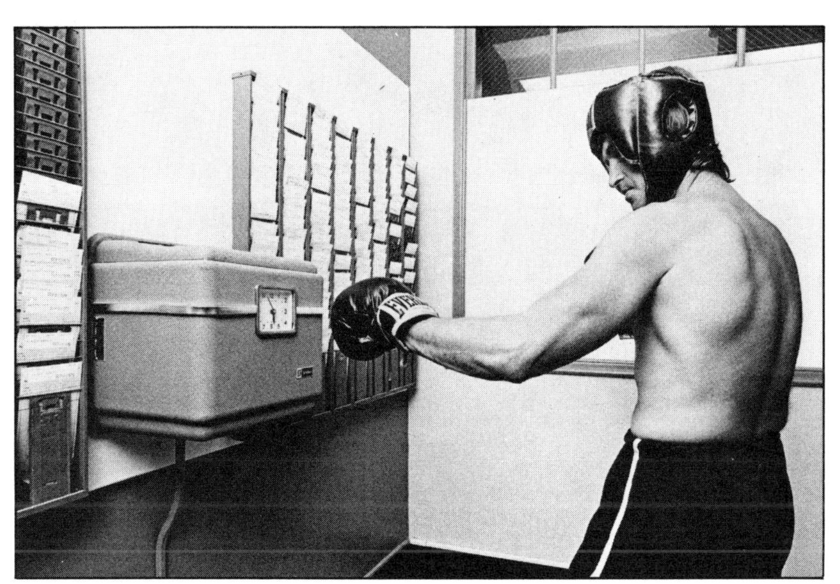

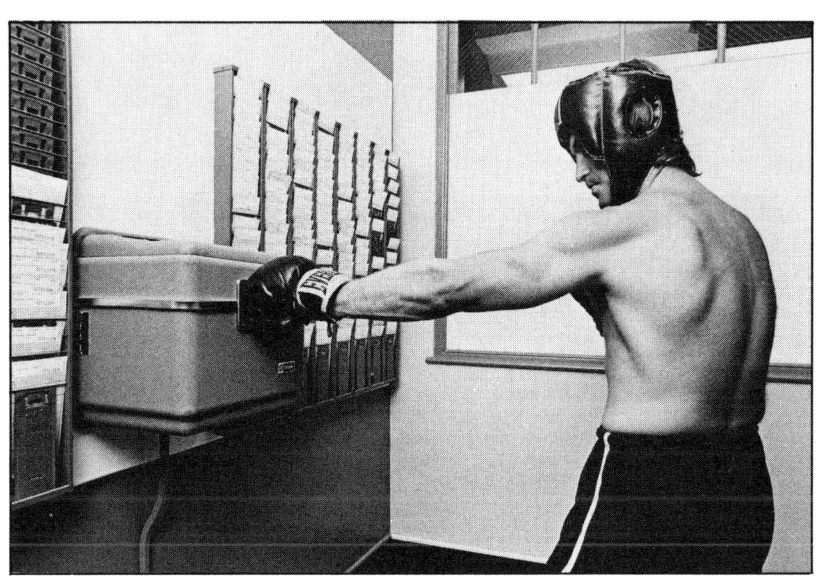

Punching a time clock

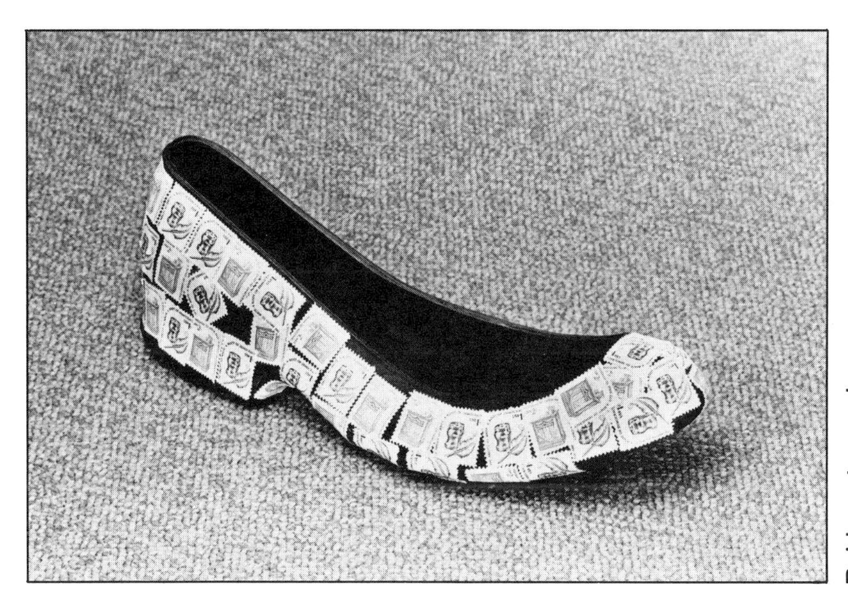

Rubber stamped

Boot camp

Bee prepared.

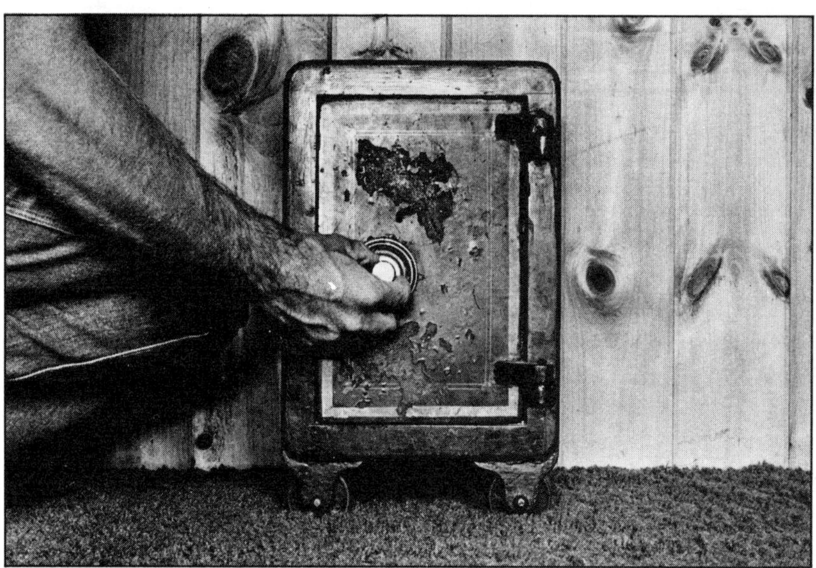

Safe crackers

Sax and violins on television

The two-knight show

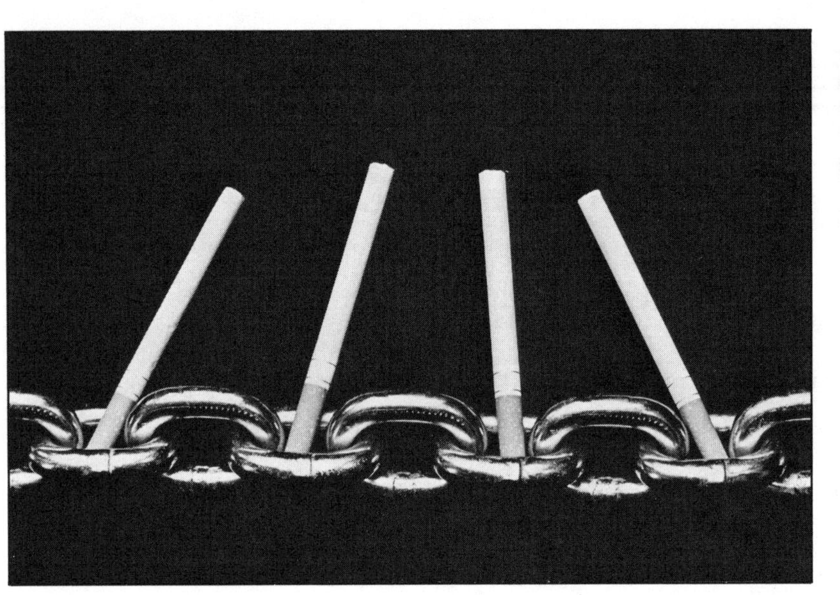

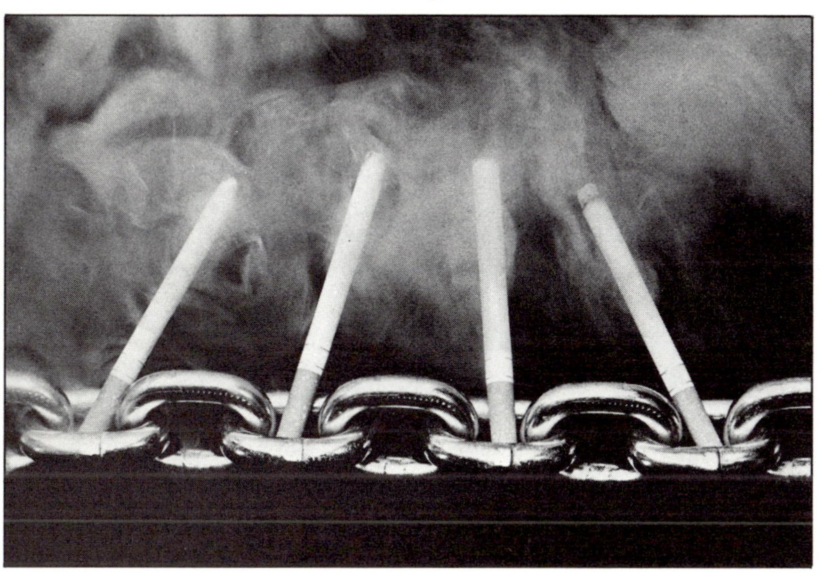

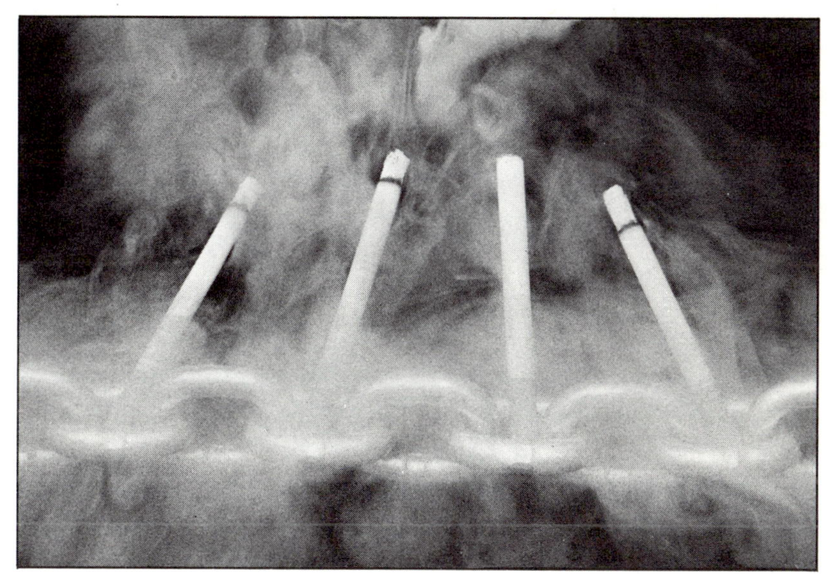

Chain smoking

A drink on the house

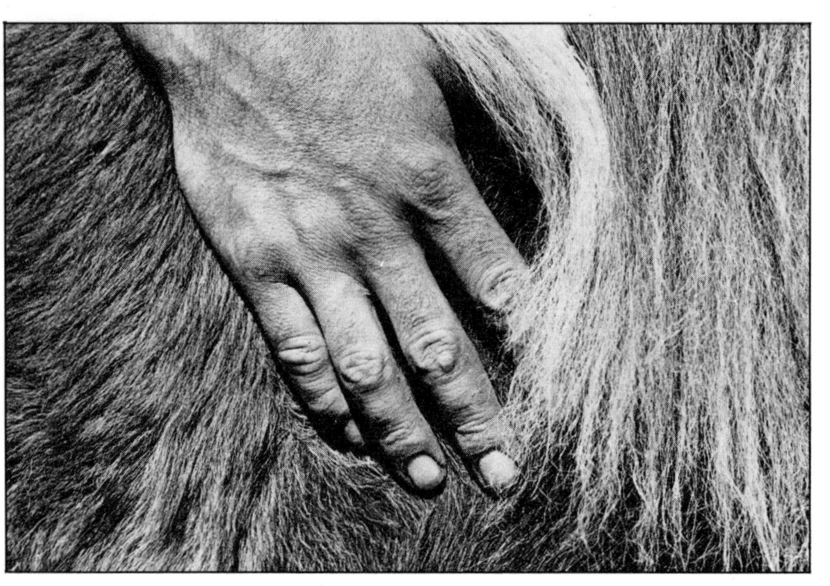

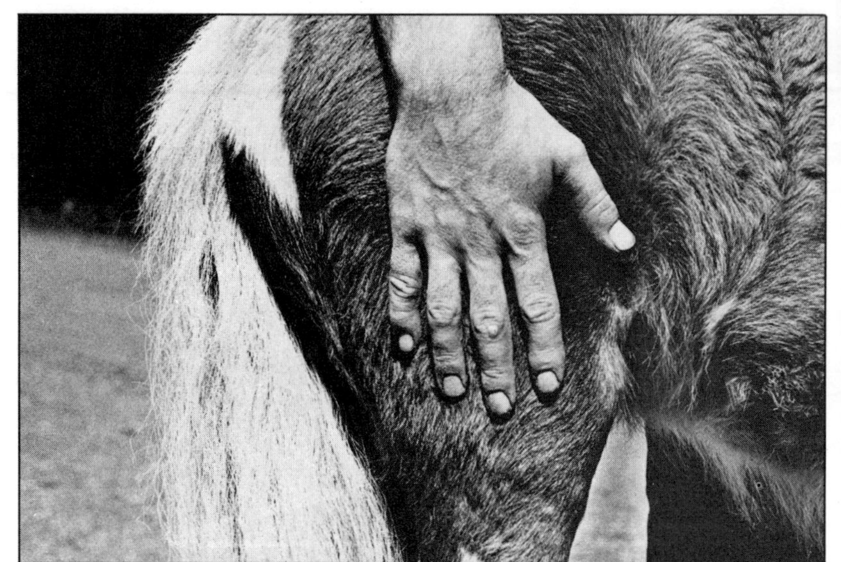

Feeling a little horse

Ass backwards

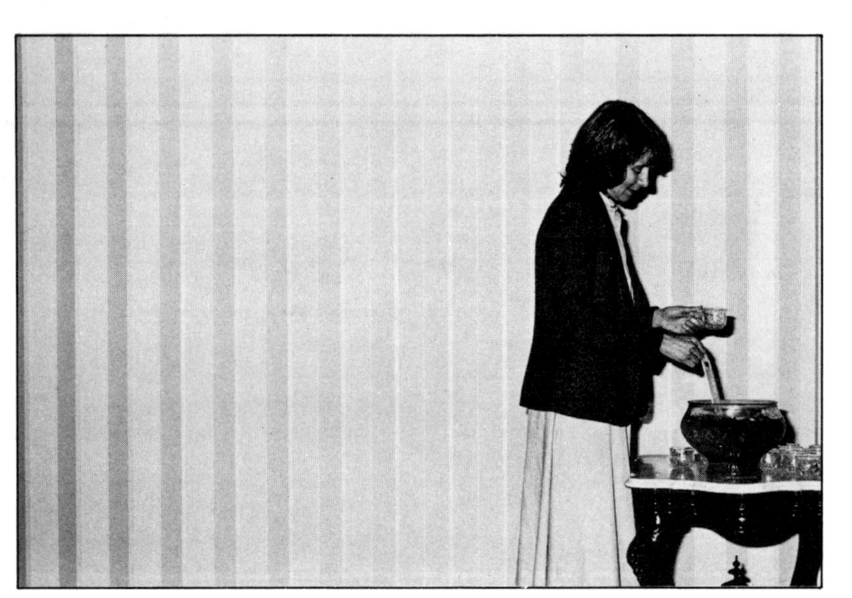

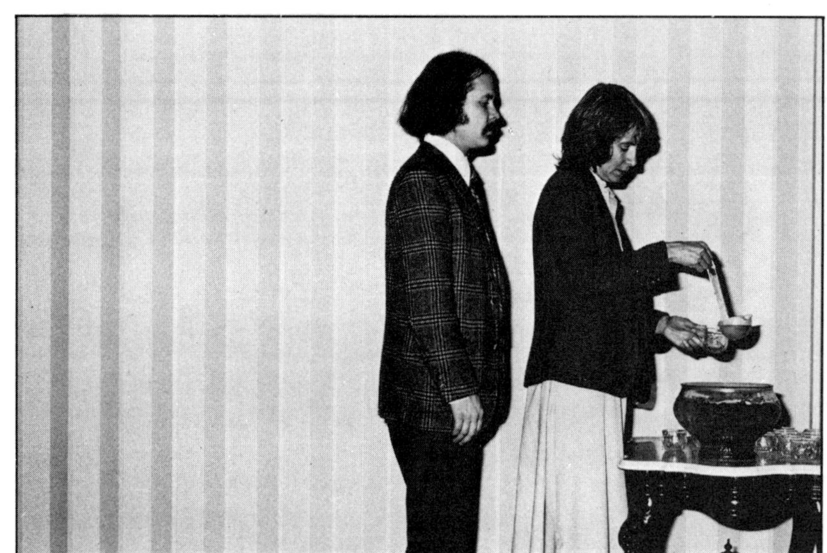

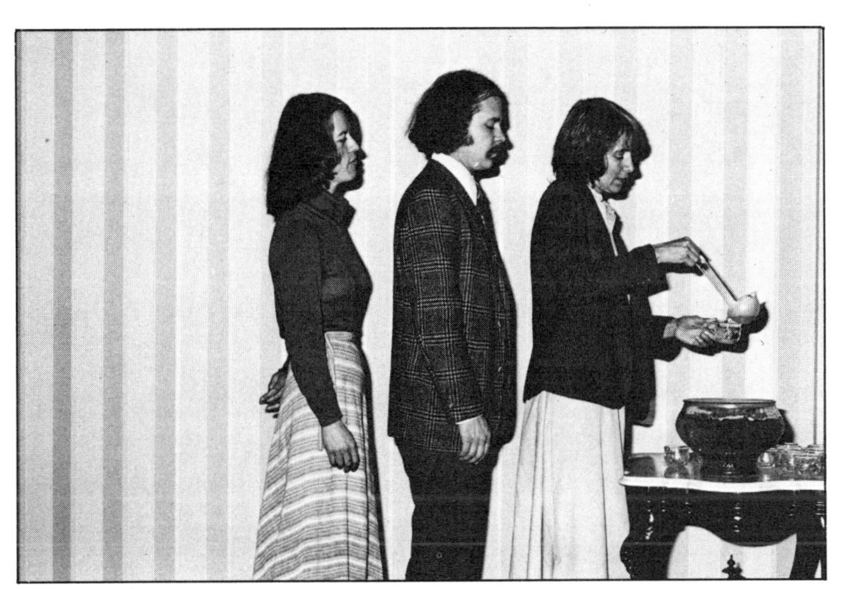

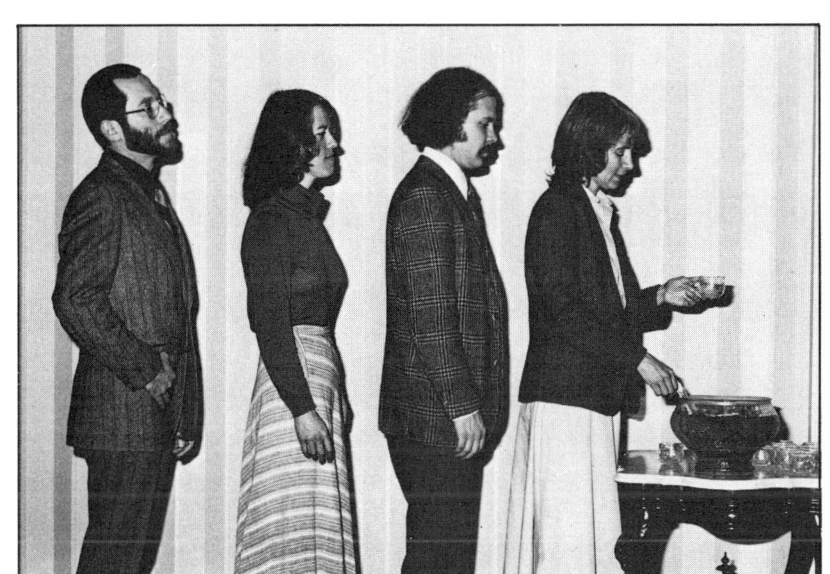

The punch line

Acknowledgments

I thank these people for their help and/or participation in photographing this book:

The Upper Story Bookstore, Springvale, Maine, for booking me.

Lawrence Cann and his line of hares that receded.

Barbara Szopa for lighting up at the Captain Lord Mansion.

Dennis Williams for reading between his lions.

Barbara Mather for beeting me, and Wayne Burbank, of Burbank's Landscaping Service, Sanford, Maine, for the bush.

Ed Loija for raising a bumper crop, making him outstanding in his field, and George Huard for his bumpy parts.

George Lavigne and Brett for not chickening out and helping me lay it on the line.

Bruce Lamb, Ed Smith, Mike Cook, and Dicky Goodwin, of the Shapleigh Volunteer Fire Department, for passing Mary Cuneo's buck.

The Springvale Hardware Store, Springvale, Maine, expecially George, Keith, and Richard, for helping me get down to brass tacks, with their ball, by smoking their chain, bit by bit by bit.

Eleanor Loija for being so frank and sharing her space, and the Cockburn family for their stein.

Bryce Bachyrycz and Julia Butterfly for going off on a tan gent, Jan Dasie.

Terr for ringing me with her carrots and then changing her tire.

Judy Brown, Doris "Dot" Brown, Brenda Goodwin, and Else-Maria Cook, of the Shapleigh Women's Auxiliary, for supporting the fire department's hose.

Svea Seredin, the belle of this ball, dressy Lauren Libby, of the Fashion Wheel, Springvale, Maine, and Linda Pence for chiming in with her bell.

Karen Moynihan, who wasn't flat busted with her sense of humor.

Gavin "Scotty" Falconer, of The Heathery House, Kennebunkport, Maine, for having his drink on the rocks.

Frank and Whit for giving me some space to rock and roll with my string quartet.

Philip St. Cyr for punching the time clock at the Henrietta Goodall Hospital, Sanford, Maine.

Tim Arsenault for the rubber to stamp.

Dana Johnson, of the Dexter Shoe Store, Sanford, Maine, for giving me the boot.

Donald Howard, just for bee-ing a good scout, and Brian Howard for the bee-coming suit.

Vinton "Wink" Ridley and family for the safe to crack, and the mystery man who crackered it.

Tom Brown for a little sax, Ben Guillemette for some violins, and Nancy and Dave Massanari for the television to put them on.

Rusty Martineau, Edward Cockburn, George Drisko, and the Sanford, Maine, High School for putting on such a show, and Frank Richards for his two knights.

Weikko, of Rauhamaa, for the house to drink on.

Michael Smith for feeling Cathy Zumbrunnen's little horse.

The Donald Walker family and their donkey, Peppy.

Norma Scott, Rev. Fred Muir, Marlene Parent, Dan Rhodes, and the Sanford, Maine, Unitarian Church for being so punchy.

TECHNICAL DATA:

Camera:	Nikon F2
Lenses:	Nikon 20mm, 35mm, 50mm, 55mm macro, 105mm, and 200mm
Light:	Available sunlight, with reflectors; Ascor 1600 II flash, bare bulb, and ringlight; tungsten spotlights, bounced; various combinations of light sources
Film/Developer:	Kodak Tri-X/Microdol-X
Paper/Developer:	Agfa Brovira, grades 3 and 4/Dektol

For a complete list of books available from Penguin in the United States, write to Dept. DG, Penguin Books, 299 Murray Hill Parkway, East Rutherford, New Jersey 07073.

For a complete list of books available from Penguin in Canada, write to Penguin Books Canada Limited, 2801 John Street, Markham, Ontario L3R 1B4.

If you live in the British Isles, write to Dept. EP, Penguin Books Ltd, Harmondsworth, Middlesex.

PUNOGRAPHY

Bruce A. McMillan

As the predecessor of the present volume, *Punography* offers a feast for the eye and a challenging brain-teaser. Photographer Bruce A. McMillan has invented the visual pun and with his camera serves up congeries of clichés in photographic form. If *Punography Too* has whetted your appetite, the original *Punography* will give you a witty, piquant repast.